THE ROYAL HORTICULTURAL SOCIETY

WILD IN THE GARDEN

DIARY
2024

FRANCES LINCOLN

First published in 2023 by Frances Lincoln Publishing,
an imprint of The Quarto Group.
1 Triptych Place, 2nd Floor, London,
SE1 9SH, United Kingdom
www.Quarto.com

A catalogue record for this book is available from the
British Library.

ISBN 978 0 7112 8299 5

10 9 8 7 6 5 4 3 2

Printed in China

RHS FLOWER SHOWS 2024

The Royal Horticultural Society holds a number of
prestigious flower shows throughout the year. At the
time of going to press, show dates for 2024 had not been
confirmed but details can be found on the website at:
rhs.org.uk/shows-events.

Every effort is made to ensure calendarial data is correct
at the time of going to press but the publisher cannot
accept any liability for any errors or changes.

Front cover: Chaffinch (*Fringilla coelebs*)
Back cover: Honey bee (*Apis mellifera*)
First page: Migrant hawker (*Aeshna mixta*)

PICTURE CREDITS

All photographs are from Shutterstock:
© **Giedriius** Front cover; **Paul Maguire** Back cover;
KPixMining Title page; **Chursina Viktoriia** Introduction;
Hawk777 Week 1; **Nelida Zubia** Week 2; **Christopher P
McLeod** Week 3; **Erni** Week 4, Week 23, Week 29, Week 51;
StevenW Wild Media Week 6; **Nigel Jarvis** Week 7; **Alexa
Zari** Week 8; **Alex Cooper Photography** Week 10; **RAY-BON**
Week 11; **SanderMeertinsPhotography** Week 12; **Sandra
Standbridge** Week 13, Week 41; **Colin Seddon** Week 15; **J
Need** Week 16; **Aragami12345s** Week 17; **Anne Coatesy**
Week 19, Week 42; **Zhukovskaya Elena** Week 20; **Stephan
Morris** Week 21, Week 35, Week 45; **Valentina Moraru**
Week 24; **Tanya_Terekhina** Week 25; **Helen J Davies** Week
26, Week 48; **Mehmetkrc** Week 28; **Marcin Rogozinski**
Week 30; **Amani A** Week 32, Week 38; **Robert Adami** Week
33; **Aaron J Hill** Week 34; **Ademortuus** Week 37; **Mark
Bridger** Week 39; **Bildagentur Zoonar GmbH** Week 43;
Ian Laker Photography Week 46; **Matt Gibson** Week 47;
Kristine Rad Week 50; **BBA Photography** Week 52.

CALENDAR 2024

JANUARY
M	T	W	T	F	S	S
	1	2	3	4	5	6	7
8	9	10	11	12	13	14
15	16	17	18	19	20	21
22	23	24	25	26	27	28
29	30	31				

FEBRUARY
M	T	W	T	F	S	S
			1	2	3	4
5	6	7	8	9	10	11
12	13	14	15	16	17	18
19	20	21	22	23	24	25
26	27	28	29			

MARCH
M	T	W	T	F	S	S
				1	2	3
4	5	6	7	8	9	10
11	12	13	14	15	16	17
18	19	20	21	22	23	24
25	26	27	28	29	30	31

APRIL
M	T	W	T	F	S	S
1	2	3	4	5	6	7
8	9	10	11	12	13	14
15	16	17	18	19	20	21
22	23	24	25	26	27	28
29	30					

MAY
M	T	W	T	F	S	S
		1	2	3	4	5
6	7	8	9	10	11	12
13	14	15	16	17	18	19
20	21	22	23	24	25	26
27	28	29	30	31		

JUNE
M	T	W	T	F	S	S
					1	2
3	4	5	6	7	8	9
10	11	12	13	14	15	16
17	18	19	20	21	22	23
24	25	26	27	28	29	30

JULY
M	T	W	T	F	S	S
1	2	3	4	5	6	7
8	9	10	11	12	13	14
15	16	17	18	19	20	21
22	23	24	25	26	27	28
29	30	31				

AUGUST
M	T	W	T	F	S	S
			1	2	3	4
5	6	7	8	9	10	11
12	13	14	15	16	17	18
19	20	21	22	23	24	25
26	27	28	29	30	31	

SEPTEMBER
M	T	W	T	F	S	S
						1
2	3	4	5	6	7	8
9	10	11	12	13	14	15
16	17	18	19	20	21	22
23	24	25	26	27	28	29
30						

OCTOBER
M	T	W	T	F	S	S
1	2	3	4	5	6
7	8	9	10	11	12	13
14	15	16	17	18	19	20
21	22	23	24	25	26	27
28	29	30	31			

NOVEMBER
M	T	W	T	F	S	S
				1	2	3
4	5	6	7	8	9	10
11	12	13	14	15	16	17
18	19	20	21	22	23	24
25	26	27	28	29	30	

DECEMBER
M	T	W	T	F	S	S
						1
2	3	4	5	6	7	8
9	10	11	12	13	14	15
16	17	18	19	20	21	22
23	24	25	26	27	28	29
30	31					

CALENDAR 2025

JANUARY
M	T	W	T	F	S	S
		1	2	3	4	5
6	7	8	9	10	11	12
13	14	15	16	17	18	19
20	21	22	23	24	25	26
27	28	29	30	31		

FEBRUARY
M	T	W	T	F	S	S
					1	2
3	4	5	6	7	8	9
10	11	12	13	14	15	16
17	18	19	20	21	22	23
24	25	26	27	28		

MARCH
M	T	W	T	F	S	S
					1	2
3	4	5	6	7	8	9
10	11	12	13	14	15	16
17	18	19	20	21	22	23
24	25	26	27	28	29	30
31						

APRIL
M	T	W	T	F	S	S
	1	2	3	4	5	6
7	8	9	10	11	12	13
14	15	16	17	18	19	20
21	22	23	24	25	26	27
28	29	30				

MAY
M	T	W	T	F	S	S
			1	2	3	4
5	6	7	8	9	10	11
12	13	14	15	16	17	18
19	20	21	22	23	24	25
26	27	28	29	30	31	

JUNE
M	T	W	T	F	S	S
						1
2	3	4	5	6	7	8
9	10	11	12	13	14	15
16	17	18	19	20	21	22
23	24	25	26	27	28	29
30						

JULY
M	T	W	T	F	S	S
	1	2	3	4	5	6
7	8	9	10	11	12	13
14	15	16	17	18	19	20
21	22	23	24	25	26	27
28	29	30	31			

AUGUST
M	T	W	T	F	S	S
				1	2	3
4	5	6	7	8	9	10
11	12	13	14	15	16	17
18	19	20	21	22	23	24
25	26	27	28	29	30	31

SEPTEMBER
M	T	W	T	F	S	S
1	2	3	4	5	6	7
8	9	10	11	12	13	14
15	16	17	18	19	20	21
22	23	24	25	26	27	28
29	30					

OCTOBER
M	T	W	T	F	S	S
		1	2	3	4	5
6	7	8	9	10	11	12
13	14	15	16	17	18	19
20	21	22	23	24	25	26
27	28	29	30	31		

NOVEMBER
M	T	W	T	F	S	S
					1	2
3	4	5	6	7	8	9
10	11	12	13	14	15	16
17	18	19	20	21	22	23
24	25	26	27	28	29	30

DECEMBER
M	T	W	T	F	S	S
1	2	3	4	5	6	7
8	9	10	11	12	13	14
15	16	17	18	19	20	21
22	23	24	25	26	27	28
29	30	31				

GARDENS AND WILDLIFE

Gardens are an important ecosystem. All ecosystems are interdependent and dynamic systems of living organisms interacting with the physical environment. Gardens by their nature are extremely variable, with a diversity of plants that can surpass that of 'natural' ecosystems. Combined with resources such as ponds and compost heaps, gardens deliver a wide variety of habitats where wildlife can thrive. Gardens provide food and a home for thousands of creatures throughout their lifecycles, and this wildlife is vital to a healthy and vibrant living garden.

The large range of garden wildlife is there because of gardening, not despite it. Gardens provide resources year-round, from overwintering sites to summer food plants. No garden or green space is too small to provide some benefit. A window box, for instance, can provide a nectar stop for bumblebees and other pollinators. The huge range of plants and kinds of garden management results in a mosaic of habitats spanning a much wider area than a single garden. Wildlife doesn't recognise our boundaries and gardens, especially those with pervious perimeters such as hedges, provide important corridors enabling the movement of mammals such as hedgehogs, birds, butterflies and other creatures.

Most gardens already support a variety of wildlife and, with a little thought and planning, they can sustain even more. Adding more plants, a pond, bird, bee and bat boxes, decaying wood, a compost heap or an undisturbed leaf pile will provide valuable habitats. The more diverse the habitats, the greater the number of species and individuals of birds, bees, bats, beetles, moths and other animals that will use a garden. The RHS recognises and actively promotes the valuable contribution that wildlife makes to gardens and gardens to wildlife. The act of gardening for wildlife can also bring great enjoyment and health benefits to gardeners. For more information visit: www.rhs.org.uk and www.wildaboutgardens.org

Great tit (*Parus major*)

'Berries provide a valuable food source for birds.'

JOBS FOR THE MONTH

- Regardless of the weather, a reliable source of unfrozen water is essential for birds for drinking and bathing, so keep bird baths topped up and ice-free.
- Scatter bird food on the ground and bird table. You can also hang bird feeders and fat balls on branches and fences, and keep them topped up. Birds follow a routine, so try to keep your feeding regime consistent if possible – this will encourage birds to regularly return to the garden.
- Make sure to clean bird baths and feeding stations regularly, as good hygiene is essential to prevent diseases. It is also a good idea to move the feeding station around every few weeks to avoid a build-up of spilt food – this can encourage less desirable visitors such as rats.

PLANT FOR WILDLIFE

- The best way to encourage wildlife into your garden is to provide a range of different habitats to support the needs of a variety of creatures in the food chain.
- Create habitats such as a pile of logs to provide shelter for small animals, or small patches of both short and long grass to allow birds easy access to grubs and worms, and lawn flowers to benefit pollinating insects. A compost heap for recycling organic garden waste will also provide a habitat for a wide range of insects and other invertebrates.
- Choose border plants so that you have something in flower every month from March to October. Leaves and seedheads can provide winter shelter for ladybirds and other invertebrates.
- Planting a tree provides a host of habitats for a wide variety of insects and other animals. Make sure to match the tree to the space as some may not be suited to urban conditions or may get too large.
- Consider planting more shrubs and trees that produce berries, as these will provide a valuable food source for birds.

JANUARY

New Year's Day
Holiday, UK, Republic of Ireland, USA, Canada,
Australia and New Zealand

Holiday, Scotland and New Zealand

Tuesday 2

Wednesday 3

Last quarter

Strip wash / clothes / pads on / hearing
aid on
BF given
Meds
Kitchen wiped   → Ore abbercare

Thursday 4

Friday 5

- settled to bed
- freshened up / nighties on / clean pad on it
- wash up
- stripped-wash. pads on. hearing aids in.
- Meds, breakfast (porridge & toast

Epiphany   *Saturday* 6

Sunday 7

JANUARY

---

8 *Monday*

---

9 *Tuesday* 11:30 HAIR - Vanessa

---

10 *Wednesday*

---

11 *Thursday* *New moon*

---

12 *Friday*

---

13 *Saturday*

---

14 *Sunday*

Small white (*Pieris rapae*)

JANUARY

Holiday, USA (Martin Luther King Jnr Day)   *Monday* **15**

Tuesday **16**

Wednesday **17**

First quarter   *Thursday* **18**

Friday **19**

Saturday **20**

Sunday **21**

Harvest mouse (*Micromys minutus*)

JANUARY

22 *Monday*

23 *Tuesday*

24 *Wednesday*

25 *Thursday*   *Full moon*

26 *Friday*   Holiday, Australia (Australia Day)

27 *Saturday*

28 *Sunday*

Redwing (*Turdus iliacus*)

'Late winter is a great time to put in a garden pond.'

JOBS FOR THE MONTH

- Put up nest boxes for birds.
- Continue to put food out for birds and keep your feeders topped up. Avoid putting out more food than can be eaten in a few days.
- Keep the bird bath topped up and free of ice as much as possible.

BIRDS IN THE GARDEN

- Common birds to see in winter include blackbirds, tits, robins and thrushes. Look out for redwings and fieldfares, too.
- At this time of year, it is more important than ever to feed the birds in your garden, as many natural sources of food, such as seeds and berries, are exhausted by this time.
- Protect birds from predators by positioning bird tables or feeders away from any areas easily accessed by cats, such a roofs, trees or fences. Placing your feeders next to prickly bushes can be a good deterrent.
- Your bird table can be a simple tray. A raised edge will retain food, and a gap in each corner will allow water to drain away and help with cleaning. Move your bird feeders around the garden regularly to avoid damaging the ground underneath.

PONDS

Late winter is a great time to put in a garden pond; you may get your first frogs and toads by spring. Even the smallest pond will attract birds, insects, newts, toads and frogs, while also providing an important water source. Here are some tips for adding a pond to your garden:

- Choose a location that gets sun for part of the day and at least one sloping side to provide easy access in and out of the water.
- Try planting around the edges or letting grass grow long to create a safe passage for animals to enter and exit the pond.
- Variety in the pond will support more diverse animal life, so try to vary the depth of the water.
- It can be helpful to include a section at the pond margin with cobbles, gravel or stones to provide easy drinking spots for bees and other pollinators.

JANUARY & FEBRUARY

Monday **29**

Tuesday **30**

Wednesday **31**

Thursday **1**

Last quarter

Friday **2**

Saturday **3**

Sunday **4**

FEBRUARY

5 *Monday*

6 *Tuesday* — Holiday, New Zealand (Waitangi Day)

7 *Wednesday*

8 *Thursday*

9 *Friday* — New moon

10 *Saturday* — Chinese New Year

11 *Sunday*

Magpie moth (*Abraxas grossulariata*)

FEBRUARY

Monday **12**

Shrove Tuesday

Tuesday **13**

Valentine's Day
Ash Wednesday

Wednesday **14**

Thursday **15**

First quarter

Friday **16**

Saturday **17**

Sunday **18**

Chaffinch (*Fringilla coelebs*) alongside a great tit (*Parus major*)

FEBRUARY

19 *Monday*   Holiday, USA (Presidents' Day)

20 *Tuesday*

21 *Wednesday*

22 *Thursday*

23 *Friday*

24 *Saturday*   Full moon

25 *Sunday*

Common frog (*Rana temporaria*)

'Insects are crucial to your garden's natural balance.'

JOBS FOR THE MONTH

- Put up nest boxes for birds. These should be hung 1–3m (3–10 ft) high on walls or trees and fitted with an entrance guard to protect them from predators. Make sure any nest boxes face the north or east, as the sun's heat can make them uninhabitable. It is also a good idea to tilt the box forward slightly to prevent rain from entering it.
- Continue to top up bird feeders. Whole peanuts should be placed in a metal mesh feeder as they can be a choking hazard for fledglings.
- Make your pond more wildlife friendly (see Week 5) and look out for amphibian spawn in the pond. Frog spawn is usually in jelly-like clumps; toad spawn is in longer individual strands; and newt eggs are laid individually on pondweed leaves and stems.

INSECTS

Insects and other invertebrates are crucial to your garden's natural balance. They are vital for nutrient recycling, helping to break down dead plant matter, and many flying insects are also pollinators.

- Make sure to weed by hand as much as possible to avoid using herbicides. Remember to leave some lawn flowers, such as dandelions, which are a valuable source of nectar and pollen.
- Ladybirds, spiders and other invertebrates find winter shelter in evergreen bushes and climbers, and among fallen leaves, dead stems and seedheads.
- A compost heap for recycling garden waste will also provide a habitat for many insects.
- Mulch beds with garden compost to help feed earthworms and maintain a healthy living soil.
- Create log, twig and rock piles to provide protection and create shelter for insects.
- March is a good time to consider building or buying a bee home for solitary bees, such as mason bees, to colonise in the spring.

FEBRUARY & MARCH

Monday **26**

Tuesday **27**

Wednesday **28**

Thursday **29**

St David's Day

Friday **1**

Saturday **2**

Last quarter

Sunday **3**

MARCH

4 *Monday*

5 *Tuesday*

6 *Wednesday*

7 *Thursday*

8 *Friday*

9 *Saturday*

10 *Sunday*

New moon
Mothering Sunday, UK and Republic of Ireland

Dunnock (*Prunella modularis*)

MARCH

Commonwealth Day
First day of Ramadân (subject to sighting of the moon)

Monday **11**

Tuesday **12**

Wednesday **13**

Thursday **14**

Friday **15**

Saturday **16**

First quarter
St Patrick's Day

Sunday **17**

Cosmos

MARCH

18 *Monday*   Holiday, Republic of Ireland and
                                          Northern Ireland (St Patrick's Day)

19 *Tuesday*

20 *Wednesday*   Vernal Equinox (Spring begins)

21 *Thursday*

22 *Friday*

23 *Saturday*

24 *Sunday*   Palm Sunday

Buff-tailed or white-tailed bumblebee (*Bombus terrestris* or *Bombus lucorum*)

MARCH

Full moon   *Monday* **25**

                                                        Tuesday **26**

                                                     Wednesday **27**

Maundy Thursday   *Thursday* **28**

Good Friday
Holiday, UK, Canada, Australia and New Zealand   *Friday* **29**

                                                       Saturday **30**

Easter Sunday
British Summer Time begins   *Sunday* **31**

Chiffchaff (*Phylloscopus collybita*)

APRIL

1 *Monday*

Easter Monday
Holiday, UK (exc. Scotland), Republic of Ireland
Australia and New Zealand

2 *Tuesday*

Last quarter

3 *Wednesday*

4 *Thursday*

5 *Friday*

6 *Saturday*

7 *Sunday*

'Keep the bird bath and feeders clean and topped up.'

BIRDS

By this time of the year, migrant birds, such as willow warblers, house martins, swifts and swallows, will have arrived from Africa. The nesting season is also well underway. The dawn chorus can be deafening as birds compete with each other for territories and mates. Swallows and spotted flycatchers will nest on suitable ledges in or on quiet outbuildings. To encourage birds to the garden, keep feeders topped up. You can buy high-quality bird food online or from retail outlets. Alternatively, you can make your own fat balls (see Week 36) using natural fats such as lard and beef suet. Plain peanut butter with no added sugar or salt also works well.

JOBS FOR THE MONTH

- Remove excess plant growth from ponds, swilling it in a bucket of pond water or leaving it on the side for 24 hours before adding it to the compost heap to allow any trapped creatures to return to the water.
- Leave out meaty cat or dog food for hedgehogs.
- Plant a hanging basket or window box to attract bees and butterflies using nasturtiums, English marigolds and lavender. Make sure to position it somewhere sunny in the garden.
- Plant annuals and perennials (single flowers as opposed to double flowers) to encourage pollinators into the garden. You can look for ideas on the RHS Plants for Pollinators lists.
- Keep the bird bath clean and topped up. In addition to any feeders, put food out on the ground, making sure to avoid chunky foods that might cause fledglings to choke.
- Stop mowing an area of lawn to allow the grass and flowers to grow. This will support a wide range of invertebrates including grasshoppers, true bugs and moth caterpillars.
- Make or buy a bat box and mount it on a sheltered but sunny wall.

APRIL

New moon   *Monday* 8

Eid al-Fitr (end of Ramadân) (subject to sighting of the moon)   *Tuesday* 9

Wednesday 10

Thursday 11

Friday 12

Saturday 13

Sunday 14

Red squirrel (*Sciurus vulgaris*)

APRIL

15 *Monday* *First quarter*

16 *Tuesday*

17 *Wednesday*

18 *Thursday*

19 *Friday*

20 *Saturday*

21 *Sunday*

Greenfinch (*Chloris chloris*

APRIL

Monday **22**

Full moon
St George's Day
First day of Passover (Pesach)

Tuesday **23**

Wednesday **24**

Holiday, Australia and New Zealand (Anzac Day)

Thursday **25**

Friday **26**

Saturday **27**

Sunday **28**

Red Admiral (*Vanessa atalanta*)

APRIL & MAY

29 *Monday*

30 *Tuesday*

1 *Wednesday*   *Last quarter*

2 *Thursday*

3 *Friday*

4 *Saturday*

5 *Sunday*

JOBS FOR THE MONTH

- Leave informal hedges untrimmed to provide food and shelter for wildlife.
- Be careful to avoid disturbing nesting birds, and never cut a hedge or shrub if you suspect birds are present.
- Sow annuals, such as cosmos, phacelia and cornflowers, to attract insects. You could also allow some of your plants to go to seed.
- Mow a path through any areas of long grass and pull out any weeds in areas sown with annual flower mixes.

'Plant a range of nectar-rich flowers to encourage butterflies into the garden.'

CHOOSING BIRD FOOD

If you want to encourage a particular species of bird into your garden, try leaving out food particular to their requirements.

- **Robins** mealworms
- **Wrens** prefer natural foods but will take fat and seed
- **Tits** insect cakes, sunflower seeds
- **Starlings** peanut cakes
- **Dunnocks** fat and small seeds on the ground
- **Goldfinches** niger seeds
- **Sparrows** sunflower heads, mealworms
- **Finches** and **nuthatches** sunflower heads
- **Thrushes** and **blackbirds** fruit such as raisins, over-ripe apples and songbird mix scattered on the ground

BUTTERFLIES

Some of the most common butterflies to see in the garden are Red Admiral, Painted Lady, Comma, Brimstone, Peacock, Green-veined White, Small White and Large White. The Small Tortoiseshell used to be commonly seen but its numbers have declined in recent years. To encourage butterflies to your garden, make sure to plant a range of nectar-rich flowers such as red valerian and asters. To support butterflies, you also need to look after the caterpillars in your garden, so research which plants will best support them.

MAY

Early Spring Bank Holiday, UK
Holiday, Republic of Ireland
Coronation Day

Monday **6**

Tuesday **7**

New moon

Wednesday **8**

Ascension Day

Thursday **9**

Friday **10**

Saturday **11**

Mother's Day, USA, Canada, Australia and New Zealand

Sunday **12**

European hedgehog (*Erinaceus europaeus*)

MAY

---

13 *Monday*

---

14 *Tuesday*

---

15 *Wednesday*   *First quarter*

---

16 *Thursday*

---

17 *Friday*

---

18 *Saturday*

---

19 *Sunday*   Whit Sunday

Honeysuckle (*Lonicera*)

MAY

Holiday, Canada (Victoria Day)   *Monday* **20**

Tuesday **21**

Wednesday **22**

Full moon   *Thursday* **23**

Friday **24**

Saturday **25**

Trinity Sunday   *Sunday* **26**

Common darter (*Sympetrum striolatum*)

MAY & JUNE

27 *Monday*

Spring Bank Holiday, UK
Holiday, USA (Memorial Day)

28 *Tuesday*

29 *Wednesday*

30 *Thursday*

Last quarter
Corpus Christi

31 *Friday*

1 *Saturday*

2 *Sunday*

JOBS FOR THE MONTH

- Continue regularly putting out food for birds, avoiding chunky foods that might cause fledglings to choke.
- Leave fledglings undisturbed if you find them on the ground – their parents are likely not far away.
- Make a bee drinker out of a plant saucer filled with pebbles and water.
- Encourage newts to breed by introducing some non-invasive, submerged, aquatic plants into your pond. Newts lay their eggs on narrow-leaved plants.
- Remove dead foliage and blooms from aquatic plants. Leave at the side of the pond for a while to allow wildlife to return to the water before adding them to the compost heap.

SPIDERS

Spiders play a key role in the garden ecosystem. As well as eating insects, they are part of the food chain and a food source for birds. To encourage spiders, avoid pesticides and plant tall flowers and dense bushes to create 'scaffolding' for spiders to build their webs on. Keep some patches of soil bare for hunting spiders to catch their prey.

'Allowing herbs to flower will encourage butterflies and bees.'

INSECTS

There are lots of insects in the garden at this time of year.
- Summer is flying ant season, so look out for these in the garden.
- There is also an abundance of hoverflies at this time of year. Adult hoverflies are pollinators and the larvae of many species feed on greenfly and other aphids.
- Social wasps can consume many plant munching invertebrates, as well as being useful flower pollinators.
- Allowing a variety of herbs, such as marjoram, mint and sage, to flower will encourage butterflies and bees.
- Avoiding the use of lawn weedkillers will allow insect life to thrive.

JUNE

Holiday, Republic of Ireland

Monday 3

Tuesday 4

Wednesday 5

New moon

Thursday 6

Friday 7

Saturday 8

Sunday 9

Wren (*Troglodytes troglodytes*)

JUNE

10 *Monday*

11 *Tuesday*

12 *Wednesday* Feast of Weeks (Shavuot)

13 *Thursday*

14 *Friday* *First quarter*

15 *Saturday*

16 *Sunday* Father's Day, UK, Republic of Ireland, USA and Canada

Great crested newt (*Triturus cristatus*)

JUNE

First day of Eid al-Adha (subject to sighting of the moon)   *Monday* **17**

Tuesday **18**

Holiday, USA (Juneteenth)   *Wednesday* **19**

Summer solstice (Summer begins)   *Thursday* **20**

Friday **21**

Full moon   *Saturday* **22**

Sunday **23**

Comma (*Polygonia c-album*)

JUNE

24 *Monday*

---

25 *Tuesday*

---

26 *Wednesday*

---

27 *Thursday*

---

28 *Friday*

Last quarter
Holiday, New Zealand (Matariki)

---

29 *Saturday*

---

30 *Sunday*

Tawny owl (*Strix aluco*)

'Many creatures, including hedgehogs, are raising young at this time of year.'

MAMMALS

Many creatures are raising young at this time of year and young mammals are beginning to explore the world beyond their homes. Hedgehogs in particular are very active, with litters usually being born in June or July. You may see or hear their parents foraging for food at night.

AMPHIBIANS

You can make ponds wildlife friendly by creating a ramp so that frogs and other wildlife can get in and out. A stack of stones, bricks or logs can all work well. Tadpoles are developing their hind legs and will be emerging from the water to seek shelter among marginal pond plants; they are very vulnerable to predators at this time of year.

JOBS FOR THE MONTH

- Construct a hedgehog feeding station for the garden, making sure to put out hedgehog food regularly. You should also check that holes in the bottom of fences haven't become blocked, so hedgehogs can freely move between gardens.
- Continue to put out food for birds regularly and keep your bird feeders topped up.
- Lawns left to grow long in May and June can be cut now, then allowed to grow long again until September. Alternatively, mow them every four weeks to allow low-growing flowers, such as daisies, selfheal and clover to flower.
- Avoid pruning hip-producing roses – these are a valuable source of food for wildlife.
- Delay hedge trimming until the end of summer to allow wildlife to nest, shelter and feed in them. You should also leave nesting birds undisturbed in garden shrubs and trees.
- Top up ponds and water features if necessary, ideally using stored rainwater. Watch out for young frogs and newts leaving the pond as they begin to move further afield.

JULY

Holiday, Canada (Canada Day)   *Monday* **1**

Tuesday **2**

Wednesday **3**

Holiday, USA (Independence Day)   *Thursday* **4**

New moon   *Friday* **5**

Saturday **6**

Sunday **7**

JULY

8 *Monday* Islamic New Year

9 *Tuesday*

10 *Wednesday*

11 *Thursday*

12 *Friday* Holiday, Northern Ireland (Battle of the Boyne)

13 *Saturday* *First quarter*

14 *Sunday*

Seven-spot ladybird (*Coccinella septempunctata*)

JULY

St Swithin's Day   *Monday* **15**

Tuesday **16**

Wednesday **17**

Thursday **18**

Friday **19**

Saturday **20**

Full moon   *Sunday* **21**

Pied flycatcher (*Ficedula hypoleuca*)

JULY

22 *Monday*

23 *Tuesday*

24 *Wednesday*

25 *Thursday*

26 *Friday*

27 *Saturday*

28 *Sunday*   *Last quarter*

Garden spider (*Araneus diadematus*)

'Late summer is the best time for evening bat watching.'

BATS

- Late summer is the best time for bat watching in the evening.
- Bats are excellent insect predators. All bats are legally protected in Britain and this extends to their roosting and hibernation sites.
- There are 17 species of bat breeding in Britain, but their numbers have declined.
  The more common species to see in the garden are the common and soprano pipistrelle, brown longeared, noctule and Daubenton's.
- Bats eat flying insects at night, including mosquitoes, moths and beetles, helping to keep a healthy balance of life in the garden.
- Garden ponds and night-flowering plants, such as evening primrose, encourage the types of insects that bats like to hunt.
- During the day bats hide in dark places, such as hollow trees, so retain old trees with cavities in the trunk where possible.

IN THE GARDEN

- Grey squirrels can be heard chattering and squealing at one another while chasing each other around the treetops.
- Bumblebees, solitary bees and hoverflies are busy collecting nectar and pollen from flowers and herb gardens.
- In late summer, butterflies like Red Admiral and Painted Lady will appreciate fallen fruit left on the ground. They are also particularly attracted to buddleja.

BIRDS

- Many adult birds are fairly secretive in late summer, hiding in cool, shady places while their feathers are replaced during the summer moult.
- In hot, dry weather many birds enjoy 'dust-bathing' as well as washing in the bird bath.
- August sees the departure of swifts, although the majority of other migrant bird species can still be found in the garden. Starlings, jackdaws and house sparrows, in particular, can be seen caring for their young in the nest.
- Install a nest box to supplement natural habitats and encourage birds to your garden. The main criteria are that the nest box is weatherproof, safe and secure.

JULY & AUGUST

Monday 29

Tuesday 30

Wednesday 31

Thursday 1

Friday 2

Saturday 3

New moon

Sunday 4

AUGUST

5 *Monday*   Holiday, Scotland and Republic of Ireland

6 *Tuesday*

7 *Wednesday*

8 *Thursday*

9 *Friday*

10 *Saturday*

11 *Sunday*

Brown hare (*Lepus europaeus*

AUGUST

First quarter

Monday 12

Tuesday 13

Wednesday 14

Thursday 15

Friday 16

Saturday 17

Sunday 18

Grove snail (*Cepaea nemoralis*)

AUGUST

19 *Monday*   *Full moon*

20 *Tuesday*

21 *Wednesday*

22 *Thursday*

23 *Friday*

24 *Saturday*

25 *Sunday*

AUGUST & SEPTEMBER

Last quarter
Summer Bank Holiday, UK (exc. Scotland)

Monday **26**

Tuesday **27**

Wednesday **28**

Thursday **29**

Friday **30**

Saturday **31**

Father's Day, Australia and New Zealand

Sunday **1**

Weasel (*Mustela nivalis*)

SEPTEMBER

2 *Monday* Holiday, USA (Labor Day
Holiday, Canada (Labour Day

3 *Tuesday* New moor

4 *Wednesday*

5 *Thursday*

6 *Friday*

7 *Saturday*

8 *Sunday* Accession of King Charles II

PREPARE FOR WINTER

Help overwintering creatures survive the cold weather by creating sheltered places in your garden, such as a log pile for beetles, making a 'bug hotel' out of hollow stems or building a hedgehog box. Even a pile of old leaves left undisturbed will provide a home for small mammals and many insects. Hedgehogs can also benefit from supplementary feeding in the autumn, helping them to survive winter. Give them special hedgehog food, or dog or cat food, but never bread and milk.

MAKE A FAT BALL

Bird food doesn't need to be expensive and you can easily make your own fat balls. It is a good idea to make these in colder weather.
1. Mix together one part fat (suet or lard work well) to two parts seed, transfer to a saucepan and gently heat, stirring until the fat melts.
2. To make fat balls, mould the seed mixture into balls using your hands. Space apart on a tray and place in the fridge to set for 24 hours.
3. Once the fat balls are solid, put out in the garden in a regular bird feeder or fat ball feeder.

'Leave some windfall apples, pears and plums for birds to feed on.'

JOBS FOR THE MONTH

- Cover the pond surface with netting to stop excessive amounts of fallen leaves from getting in.
- Continue to top up bird feeders and put food on bird tables and on the ground. Leave some windfall apples, pears and plums for birds to feed on.
- As we come to the end of the nesting season, hedge trimming can resume – but delay for another month if you suspect birds are still active.
- Dead head flowers to encourage them to produce more blooms and pollen for insects.
- Allow seedheads to develop on some plants as a food source. Don't trim any bushes with developing berries, such as holly, cotoneaster and pyracantha.
- Give meadows a final cut before winter. Leave the clippings to lie for a couple of days before removing. This will allow wildflower seeds to fall to the ground and replenish the meadow.

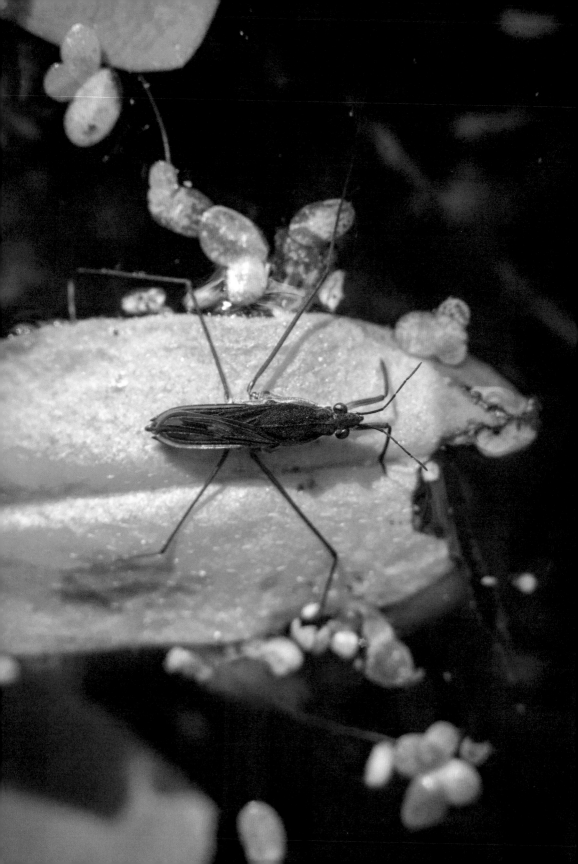

SEPTEMBER

Monday **9**

Tuesday **10**

First quarter   *Wednesday* **11**

Thursday **12**

Friday **13**

Saturday **14**

Sunday **15**

Common pond skater (*Gerris lacustris*)

SEPTEMBER

16 *Monday*

17 *Tuesday*

18 *Wednesday* *Full moon*

19 *Thursday*

20 *Friday*

21 *Saturday*

22 *Sunday* Autumnal Equinox (Autumn begins

Stonechat (*Saxicola rubicola*

SEPTEMBER

Monday **23**

Last quarter

Tuesday **24**

Wednesday **25**

Thursday **26**

Friday **27**

Saturday **28**

Michaelmas Day

Sunday **29**

Red fox (*Vulpes vulpes*)

SEPTEMBER & OCTOBER

30 *Monday*

1 *Tuesday*

2 *Wednesday*   *New moon*

3 *Thursday*   Jewish New Year (Rosh Hashanah)

4 *Friday*

5 *Saturday*

6 *Sunday*

'Leave seedheads standing to provide food and shelter for wildlife.'

JOBS FOR THE MONTH

- Avoid disturbing butterflies, such as Peacocks, which overwinter in garden buildings.
- Be careful when turning over compost heaps, as frogs, toads and other small animals may be sheltering there.
- If possible, allow uncut ivy to flower as it is an excellent late nectar source for pollinating insects and the berries last well into winter to feed birds.
- Autumn daisies are a good source of food for butterflies and bees, particularly when there are few other plants for them to feed on.
- Leave herbaceous and hollow stemmed plants unpruned until early spring to provide homes for overwintering insects.
- Clean the bird bath regularly and ensure that it is topped up with fresh water.
- Where possible, leave seedheads standing to provide food and shelter for wildlife.

BIRDS

- Winter migrant birds start to arrive from colder, northern regions. Starlings gather in large groups, and look out for redwings, bramblings and fieldfares, too.
- Top up bird feeders and put food out on the ground and bird tables, but don't be surprised if your feeder is untouched. Birds will still be foraging for natural food, such as holly berries. Whole peanuts are now safe to put out, as the breeding season is over.

MAMMALS

Foxes may become more inquisitive as natural food sources start to dwindle, so always secure your bins. Hedgehogs start preparing for hibernation so it is a good idea to put out food and water for them in the autumn. During mild spells, they can emerge from hibernation to forage for food, before returning to their hiding places as the temperature drops. Only leave hedgehog food out during the winter months if it is being taken, but continue to provide a source of clean, fresh water and be careful that it doesn't freeze over.

OCTOBER

Monday 7

Tuesday 8

Wednesday 9

First quarter   *Thursday* 10

Friday 11

Day of Atonement (Yom Kippur)   *Saturday* 12

Sunday 13

Yellow-tail moth caterpillar (*Euproctis similis*)

OCTOBER

14 *Monday*   Holiday, USA (Columbus Day)
                                                   Holiday, Canada (Thanksgiving)

15 *Tuesday*

16 *Wednesday*

17 *Thursday*   *Full moon*
                                           First day of Tabernacles (Succoth)

18 *Friday*

19 *Saturday*

20 *Sunday*

Eurasian badger (*Meles meles*)

OCTOBER

Monday 21

Tuesday 22

Wednesday 23

Last quarter

Thursday 24

Friday 25

Saturday 26

British Summer Time ends

Sunday 27

Sparrowhawk (*Accipiter nisus*)

OCTOBER & NOVEMBER

28 *Monday*

Holiday, Republic of Ireland
Holiday, New Zealand (Labour Day)

29 *Tuesday*

30 *Wednesday*

31 *Thursday*

Halloween

1 *Friday*

All Saints' Day
New moon

2 *Saturday*

3 *Sunday*

'Make a leaf pile for overwintering animals.'

JOBS FOR THE MONTH

- Empty and clean out nest boxes using boiling water. When they are thoroughly dry, place a handful of wood shavings inside to provide winter shelter.
- Animals still need access to water for drinking, so melt a hole in ice at the edge of a pond by filling a saucepan with hot water and sitting it on the ice until a hole has melted. Never crack or hit the ice as the shock waves created can harm wildlife.
- Use woody prunings to make a dead hedge and consider options other than a bonfire for disposing of garden waste. If you do have a bonfire, always check for animals before lighting.
- Regularly shake off leaves from protective nets over ponds and rake out the leaves that are not netted.
- Make a leaf pile for overwintering animals and retain fallen leaves at the base of hedges for blackbirds and thrushes to hunt through for invertebrates.
- Now is the time to make sure you are putting out high fat foods for birds, such as peanut cake and fat balls (see Week 36). Wrens and other small birds appreciate finely chopped bacon rind and grated cheese.

MOTHS

- There are over 2,500 species of moths in Britain and they play an important role in all ecosystems, including healthy gardens.
- Adult moths and their caterpillars are a key food source for various animals including hedgehogs, spiders, frogs, bats and birds. Day-flying and night-flying moths act as plant pollinators.
- To encourage moths into your garden, leave longer grasses, knapweeds and thistles in the garden, and leave hedges untrimmed if possible. It is best to tolerate caterpillar feeding damage to plants.
- Planting evergreen shrubs will provide overwintering sites for butterflies and moths.
- Planting birch, hornbeam, hawthorn, lady's bedstraw, willow and rowan will help support moth caterpillars.
- Planting common jasmine, sweet rocket, *Lychnis* and sea lavender will attract day-flying moths and many other pollinators.
- Night-flowering, nectar-rich plants will attract nocturnal moths to your garden.

NOVEMBER

Monday **4**

Guy Fawkes Night

Tuesday **5**

Wednesday **6**

Thursday **7**

Friday **8**

First quarter

Saturday **9**

Remembrance Sunday

Sunday **10**

Eurasian otter (*Lutra lutra*)

NOVEMBER

11 *Monday*

Holiday, USA (Veterans Day)
Holiday, Canada (Remembrance Day)

12 *Tuesday*

13 *Wednesday*

14 *Thursday*

Birthday of King Charles III

15 *Friday*

Full moon

16 *Saturday*

17 *Sunday*

Honey bee (*Apis mellifera*)

NOVEMBER

Monday **18**

Tuesday **19**

Wednesday **20**

Thursday **21**

Friday **22**

Last quarter

Saturday **23**

Sunday **24**

Coal tit (*Periparus ater*)

NOVEMBER & DECEMBER

25 *Monday*

26 *Tuesday*

27 *Wednesday*

28 *Thursday*

Holiday, USA (Thanksgiving)

29 *Friday*

30 *Saturday*

St Andrew's Day

1 *Sunday*

New moon
First Sunday in Advent

European rabbit (*Oryctolagus cuniculus*)

'Make a wildlife-friendly wreath out of garden moss, holly leaves and ivy.'

CHRISTMAS DECORATIONS

Making your own Christmas wreath is a fun way to get into the Christmas spirit.

- Holly berries are a valuable food source for birds, so think twice before using them in any Christmas decorations.
- Make a wildlife-friendly wreath for your front door out of garden moss, holly leaves and ivy. You could also use spruce and pine, or experiment with box, *Magnolia grandiflora*, osmanthus, *Viburnum tinus* and bay.
- For a more rustic wreath, use twisted stems of hazel, birch, dogwood, willow, honeysuckle and vines and decorate with rose hips.
- Wreaths positioned outdoors will last four or five weeks. Indoor wreaths will look fresh for one or two weeks, depending on how warm it is.

JOBS FOR THE MONTH

- Keep the bird bath topped up, clean and ice-free.
- Make sure to put out food for birds regularly, so they don't waste vital energy on visiting when there's no food available.
- Mulch vegetable beds with garden compost but delay cutting back borders until late winter, to provide shelter for invertebrates.
- Plant hedges, single-flowered roses and fruit trees to offer plenty of resources for wildlife, including blossom and fruit.
- Take care when pruning, as butterflies and moths overwinter in places that are sheltered from wind, frost and rain. They favour a thick tangle of leaves and stems, but some will use sheds or garages.

DECEMBER

Holiday, Scotland (St Andrew's Day)

Monday 2

Tuesday 3

Wednesday 4

Thursday 5

Friday 6

Saturday 7

First quarter

Sunday 8

DECEMBER

9 *Monday*

10 *Tuesday*

11 *Wednesday*

12 *Thursday*

13 *Friday*

14 *Saturday*

15 *Sunday*

Full moon

Two-spot ladybird (*Adalia bipunctata*) on a flowering plum tree (*Prunus domestica*)

DECEMBER

Monday **16**

Tuesday **17**

Wednesday **18**

Thursday **19**

Friday **20**

Winter Solstice (Winter begins)   *Saturday* **21**

Last quarter   *Sunday* **22**

Song thrush (*Turdus philomelos*)

DECEMBER

23 *Monday*

24 *Tuesday*

Christmas Eve

25 *Wednesday*

Christmas Day
Holiday, UK, Republic of Ireland, USA,
Canada, Australia and New Zealand
Hanukkah begins (at sunset)

26 *Thursday*

Boxing Day (St Stephen's Day)
Holiday, UK, Republic of Ireland, USA,
Canada, Australia and New Zealand

27 *Friday*

28 *Saturday*

29 *Sunday*

Red squirrel (*Sciurus vulgaris*)

DECEMBER & JANUARY

New moon

Monday **30**

New Year's Eve

Tuesday **31**

New Year's Day
Holiday, UK, Republic of Ireland, USA, Canada,
Australia and New Zealand

Wednesday **1**

Holiday, Scotland and New Zealand
Hanukkah ends

Thursday **2**

Friday **3**

Saturday **4**

Sunday **5**

Brambling (*Fringilla montifringilla*)

YEAR PLANNER

JANUARY	JULY
FEBRUARY	AUGUST
MARCH	SEPTEMBER
APRIL	OCTOBER
MAY	NOVEMBER
JUNE	DECEMBER